W9-BCI-296

DISCARDED
Mead Public Library

keepper
CR 3/01

IT'S WINTER!

IT'S WINTER!

Text
and
Photographs
by
SISTER NOEMI WEYGANT, O.S.B.

THE WESTMINSTER PRESS
Philadelphia

STANDARD BOOK No. 664-32448-7

LIBRARY OF CONGRESS CATALOG CARD No. 71-75650

BOOK DESIGN BY

DOROTHY ALDEN SMITH

Published by The Westminster Press ®
Philadelphia, Pennsylvania

PRINTED IN THE UNITED STATES OF AMERICA

CONTENTS

JOYFUL TO THE CHIN

ABOUT ten years ago I received a letter from a Benedictine
nun in Duluth who said that a book of mine about my
Colorado boyhood recalled her own pioneer childhood in
Montana. Thus a correspondence with Sister Noemi Weygant began. In an early letter I asked about the Benedictine
Order, and she said its purpose was nursing and teaching,
and added, "My teaching is with pictures." She was a pho-
tographer. But in the same letter she sent a poem about buttercups for Barbara, my wife. And over the years I have
found that Sister Noemi has an exuberant love of life that
tries to embrace and exalt the whole outdoor world with any
means of expression at hand—poems, prose, or pictures.

Primarily she is a poet with a camera. One winter she sent
us a packet of breathtaking pictures of snow and ice. She had
been sick, housebound, but with the pictures was a note: "I
was outside today and I came in joyful to the chin! The snow
glitters, the fields are waltzing in the sun, and every weed is
glorified."

I wonder if that wasn't the day she first thought of this
book. Only a few days later she wrote, "I have had a jaunt
in the winter woodlands and came back all snow-laden on
sweater and boots." And a little later, "I must write, I must
make my pictures! Of trees and buttercups, and ice and snow
and summer and spring and every season!"

That is what she has done. She has glorified the world she
loves with words and pictures, and here is her winter book.
Its poems and pictures are clearly a part of each other, and
both are a part of her. They celebrate the winter world with
such skill and truth and yet so simply that the art escapes
naïveté by a wisp. But it does escape, and that's the miracle,
the magic. How she does it, I don't know; but here it is, rare,
total, and ageless. And now we, too, can know Sister Noemi's
winter world and be "joyful to the chin."

Hal Borland

STEP QUIETLY

Together,
   let us go out-of-doors
      to explore.

Step quietly
   in this woodland hall
      and don't talk.

On skis,
   snowshoes,
      or merely in overshoes,
   happy,
      step into winter.

WINTER IS TACKED DOWN

Hurrah!

Hurray!

It snowed last night.

Today
   the green lawn
      is whiskered with white.

Look around—
   enough snow on the ground
      for a snowball.

Scoop it up in your hands,
   gloves or no.
Wad it,
   pack it tight,
      round,
       big.

Let go!

Smash!
Splash!

Winter is here!

You can't hold winter back,
   not possibly,
      once you have tacked a snowball
      to the trunk of a tree.

HOW DOES WINTER DO IT?

Winter can take
   a good-for-nothing
   summer something
    and make it
    into a dancer.

A fieldful of weeds,
   many and varied,
    will seem to be flowing
  in exotic rhythm
    to the music
    of wind blowing
    over snow.

ONE OF WINTER'S TOYS

Winter is forever making toys
    out of things that are of no use
        to anyone else—
    a tin can,
    a plastic bottle,
    an inner tube,
    a rusty wheel.
Here we find winter has designed
    a bridge.
Over it imaginary cars
    and engines
        are running.

Hear them puff-poofing,
    toot-hooting,
    honk-cronking.

Suddenly,
    the silver bridge quivers.
        Tinkling,
        tumbling,
        sliding,
                        down it goes.

But winter doesn't care.
She's had her play with it.

Another day,
    using ice for glue
    and snow for clay,
    winter will build another bridge,
        somewhere else,
        some other way.

HE LIVES IN A TREE

More animals
   than you would believe
   live in trees
    in winter.
Many of them,
   so far as I know,
   have no names,
   and disappear
    in the next
    big blow.

What creature is this?

A bear?

A seal?

Does he have a tail?

Can he be
   a humpback whale?

Does he bite,
   bark,
   growl,
   spout?

His fur must be very thick
   or the needles of his bed would prick.

I BOAST

A nature book
　　will tell you
　　there are more than
　　six thousand species
　　　of earthworm.

But I can boast
　　that not one scientist
　　in all the world
　　　has classified me,
　　though I am winter's one and only worm.

THEY WERE SO COLD

Winter came one year
   before the fall berries
   had been put away
     out of the cold.
They complained
   bitterly.

When winter heard of their plight
   she stayed
   up all night
   to knit warm white caps,
     fitting each little red head neatly
     before going to bed.

Now the berries,
   wearing their caps,
     call out to all
     who pass by,

"See!

How warm!

How pretty!"

WINTER ART

Winter,
    with wet and freeze,
    makes everything
    autumn threw away
        into a masterpiece.

It took only one night
    to create
    this candle holder,
        wax dripping,
        bright.

But winter is jealous
    of her art.
If you try to take it home,
    rather than part
    with it,
        she will make
        it break.

So going through
    a winter garden
    or a forest
        is something like
        visiting a museum—

    Nothing to be touched,
        but everything free
        for you to see.

23

ALL IN ONE NIGHT

There is an old fence
    in the backyard,
        rusty and bent.

But this morning,
    between the wire framing,
    on leaf and stem
        fresh flowers are growing.
Or are they winter's feathers
    blown and caught?

BEWARE . . . MAYBE!

Halt!
Another step
   and you may have your foot
      on the back
      of a porcupine.

His quiver
   is full of arrows,
      and he might . . . let go!

On the other hand,
   maybe this is
   only another of winter's tricks,
   for winter can be a magician,
      a comedian,
      or
      a great big fibber.

RESCUE ME

Am I the ghost
   of a horse
   that used to be,
   left hanging
   on this tree
      by winter?
Or was I deserted here
   by my rider?

Quickly,
   before the sun
   begins
   to shine again,

      rescue me.

GO AWAY

When children
  trample
    through the gardens,
flowers
and other plants
waiting for spring
  have no voices
  to cry out—
  "Help!"

But winter has a way,
  with thorns and ice,
    sharp and cold,
  to make the children go
somewhere else
  for a snow fight.

31

I DANCE . . . I DANCE

I dance
  with white fire
  blowing thin
    in winter wind.
My stage
  is so narrow
  and slippery
  the slightest mistake
  in toeing
    would be
    the death of me.

Behind me is a curtain
  bluer than the ocean.

I dance,

  I dance,

    I dance,

  to the whims of thaw and freeze
    from the top of one
    snowbank to another.

Then comes spring,
  and puts out my cold fire.

THE GOLDEN TRIANGLE

In school
 you learn to play
  a triangle
 by striking it
  with a mallet,
 but the note is always metallic.

In the forest
 there is a wild green reed
  that grows very tall.

Then comes the first frost
 to turn the reed gold,
 shape it into a triangle,
  and provide a mallet.

But to play
 this particular
 musical instrument
  requires
  a very special talent

  and only winter has it!

CAREFUL!

The day is so bright,
   my head is so light,

oh,

I long to romp and bark and play—

but if I do,
   oh, woe to you
   and woe to me.

Even a toss of my head,
   and it will be

      SMITHEREENS.

BOW BEFORE HIM

In the dark deep
   of the forest,
      on ermine snow,
   a royal bird holds court,
      with outstretched wings
      of brown and gold.
He is not
   the least afraid
      or he would fly away.

But . . . why should he?

For in his imperial forest
   he is Emperor.

THE WILD EYE

I'm scared!
See that wild eye
  glaring at us.

What monster
  of an animal
    hides behind the snowbank?

Before he makes a plunge . . .

                    Run!

SAYS A WINTER CRICKET

It is written
  of the snowy tree cricket
  that it dies
    with the coming
    of cold weather.

But this cricket says,
"Here I am,
  bigger than .ever.
I am not wearing
  my green summer coat,
  because
    winter requires my white one.

I will admit,
  ice wings
    are heavy,
  but I have discovered
  that when I need a ride
  I can always slide
    down a snowbank."

WHEN THE WIND BLOWS

I may look lacy,
   but my shell is
plastic hard,
    and I'm tied
    to the side
    of a crib.

For I am winter's
   baby rattle,
    used to pacify
    little wild animals
   who cry
    when the wind blows . . .
              cold.

THE BULLFIGHT

Winter must be preparing
    for a bullfight!
Here is a ring
    big enough
        for a big bull's nose.
Look out—
    his fury
        will soon blow
        all the snow away.

Since the arena
    seems to be glazed,
        no doubt
    both bull and fighter
        will wear skates
        like hockey players.

What a fight
    it will be!
And
    on a school day too!

HE IS HIDING

One cold winter day
  I was walking alone
  in the heavy forest
    when a bird
     began to sing.

I stopped
  and turned round and round,
    trying to see him.

He was so hidden
  I began to wonder
  if the woodland
  was haunted
    by a spirit bird . . .

But no—
  the song
    was too strong.

And then I found him
  in silhouette,
    black as the thicket
    that sheltered him.

FOLLOW — FOLLOW

Come here! Come here!

See what I've found
  in the snow—
    the hoofprints
    of a deer?

Let us follow, follow,
  and track him down.

Under a tree,
  around a stone,
  out in the sun.
    through a shadow.

Very soon
  we ought to see him.

Suddenly, nothing!
The tracks have vanished.

Oh, hurry to the right.
Hurry to the left,
  under the brush.

Find him,
  find him.
Where?

Oh, wild deer,
  do you have wings?
Did you climb a tree?
Or did you leap a deep valley?

THE EAGLE

The eagle
　is a king
　　in the world
　　of birds
　　and mountain heights.

And so,
　is it not right
　that winter
　should so perfectly
　sculpture an eagle
　　in ice?

WE HAVE FORGOTTEN

We have forgotten
   what garden vegetable
      we were meant to be,
   for a farmer
   abandoned us
      to the will of winter,
   and the cold
   caused our memories
      to fail.

Now we stand
   like a village of tepees,
      and if we hear correctly,
      our name is . . .

         kohlrabi.

WATCH OUT!

Winter turns trees
   into ghosts,
   giants,
   scorpions,
    and hosts
    of other things.
So
   it is not surprising
   that a big branch here
    is springing out
    in a wildcat leap.

But don't be afraid.

Next summer he'll be so tame
   you can play in his shade.

FOR THE HOLY DAY

Beside the stone steps
   at the corner of the house
   summer grew some weeds
     that autumn filled
     with leaves turned brown.
Winter covered them with frozen snow,
   and shaped a Christmas wreath
     for the holy day.

FOREST STARS

Even without
   people about,
   the forest trims
   its Christmas tree
     by pinning stars
     to the tips of a pine.
There against the curtain
   of a blue winter sky
   they shine
     until they burn themselves out.

61

HUSH! WINTER IS LEAVING

There is one day
   at the end of winter
   when you discover
   that the last of the snow
   has melted.
Every little hollow,
   like a blue bowl,
   holds water,
   cold,
     and catches raindrops
     from a dripping sky.

The woods are still.
Even the crow, the squirrel,
   all wild animals and birds,
     are hidden, silent . . .

               Why?

Winter, which took
   good care
     of the fields and forests,
   is leaving them now
     with a prayer.

So . . . Hush! Wait!

Within a week or two,
   shiny,
   warm,
   singing,
green—
               spring!